Seeing

for Janet, who asked the question

Seeing the River

Raymond Friel

Polygon
EDINBURGH

Published by Polygon
22 George Square
Edinburgh

Set in Sabon by Koinonia Ltd,
Manchester
Printed and bound in Great Britain by
Short Run Press Ltd, Exeter

A CIP record is available

ISBN 0 7486 6195 6

The Publisher acknowledges subsidy from

THE SCOTTISH ARTS COUNCIL

towards the production of this volume.

and the smell of a resurrection
arrived through the shirts
when the washing was left out all night
in the water and blackness.

John Burnside, 'R.E.'

Acknowledgements

Acknowledgment is gratefully made to the editors of the following periodicals and anthologies in which poems, or earlier versions, have appeared: *New Writing Scotland 7, 9, 10, 11, Gairfish, Verse, Lines Review, West Coast Magazine, Northwords, Spectrum, Understanding* and *London Review of Books.*

A number of these poems are published in *Bel-Air* (Southfields Press, London, 1993) and in *Dream State: The New Scottish Poets* (Polygon, Edinburgh, 1994).

The ships' names in 'Davydeep' come from *Clyde Shipwrecks* by Peter Moir and Ian Crawford (Moir & Crawford, Wemyss Bay, 1988).

Special thanks to Richard Price, for his friendship and critical eye.

Contents

OUT OF THE DEPTHS

In the cold churches
Of my childhood,
Imagination shoaled
In sonar depths.

Razorbills, perched
On sculpted lecterns,
Preached fire and mortal sin,
Poised to bear down

On any hint of flesh
In the murky deep:
'In bed, join your hands
And think on your death.'

I lay in darkness,
The ocean raising its chorus;
My small hands
Moving shyly...

MAY 1967

From my Olympian view
Of the Subbuteo pitch

(Tonight, left to play on
Past bedtime)

I plotted the brilliant
Jinking run and chip

That would clinch it for Scotland
In the dying seconds.

Dad roared
And leapt over me

Towards the TV,
Out of his mind:

'YEAAHSS! YA BEAUTY!'
(Chalmers had scored.)

Whimpering, I ran
For cover

To my mother's plaid hemline,
Having yet to learn

The depth and violence
Of the beautiful game.

SCHOOLDAYS

A soaked-to-the-skin wait
In the motley tail-end
That made up the numbers,
Then told to go and defend.

My big news at tea-time
Was that I *got a kick* –
A short-lived toe-ender
In the goalmouth panic.

But some of them had style:
Chesting it down, past
One and angled in off the bin,
Raising a nonchalant fist.

A po-faced Miss Pinelli,
Clean page and today's date;
Hands aching to record
Some boozed-up empire's fate.

The projects, more fun,
Like The Industrial Age –
The Use of Child Labour
A stick boy on the page.

McCreary, the hard man,
Blurting out 'I hate this!'
Collared out to the front,
Still defiant, 'What *Miss*?'

One time he called her a cow:
God, the scattering of chairs

As she raced after him out
The door to riotous cheers...

But dead comfy up the back,
I could usually retreat
Into pure vacancy and stare
Down at Cartsburn Street –

Where the heavy-booted men
Came drawn by the siren,
A shuffling procession
Into forests of iron.

ARISTOCRAT

A bored Sunday afternoon.
Drill of the bell. A raucous 'Hi!'
Startled the landing. 'Eh, hi.'
A long-lost relative
From the States, over in Scotland
To research *all* her family.

We found her coffee and sat
To hear the whole story;
Her long, languidly-moved hands
Tracing lines in the air.
Her perfume filled the room.
I thought she was famous.

We listened in polite
Silence: apparently,
A great-great-great somebody,
A servant girl, had a child
By a German aristocrat.
Blue blood, then, in East Crawford St!

We dug out the old albums,
Given to me, prodded
To take them over. 'All *right*' –
Making connections – 'so
This is... yeah, those *blue* eyes.
(I went to check later.)

Then she simply *had* to take
Some photographs, so down
We all went to the back-green
(Get some ambience). There

The four of us posed patiently;
Me at the front, changed. A young lord.

FIRST COMMUNION

Church bells doing their nut
In the brittle morning.
Fags lit deep in jackets.
A silver coin, cold in my palm.

Where's uncle Tommy gone?
Dabbed wetly round the mouth,
And shooshed from questions in-
to an air of solemnity:

The organ sonorous,
The altar bushed with flowers;
Miss Day: *For goodness sake*
ENUNCIATE! Now after three...

'Grace danced' was the chorus.
I didn't understand.
The plate dunted my throat;
The priest's hand, trembling. *Amen.*

It tasted like paper.
Now say your thanksgiving
Into yourself: Sweet Jesus...
How did it go again?
Sweet Jesus...

ROLE MODEL

Elvis in Las Vegas sideburns,
Dog collar and turned up leather jacket...

Summer's noonday mass
Saw an outbreak of black fever –
Temperatures rising in the roped-off gallery
As the king, in dove-emblazoned chasuble,
Genuflected on the Persian-rugged marble
To a clash of cymbals and a thousand voices
Swaying to *Kumbayah*.

He knew the score at the announcements
When he cracked his little smiling jokes
Into the swan-neck microphone, thrumming
A hee-*haw* on his snakeskin-strapped
Twelve-string Ovation; a frisson
As old as Paul to the Corinthians
Was visiting the faithful.
I wanted to be him.

Trembly, he took me
Between his knees in the sacristy
And clutched my arms. Up close,
His hazel eyes were rheumy, kind; his bristle
Flecked with grey. He said the spirit was higher
Than the law and swung a playful jab
Up to my chin. He called me a star
And patted me back to Mum saying
I'd be the next Bishop of Paisley!
And I believed him.

JANUARY 1977

The Scotch firs
Pogoed behind us
Like concert footage
Of the Sex Pistols.

Squatting on the sledge,
Dermy and I booed
At the distant all-in
From the college tower.

On top of him after three steps,
We aimed for the stile;
His bum clenched
Under my limp weight.

We skidded into
The stone wall; disen-
tangled, he punched me, once,
On the mouth;

And wouldn't catch my eye
At evening prayer:
His cheeks beetroot,
Hair spiky from the shower.

DERMY'S DAY

On days out,
Waiting for the bus,
We slouched on the stone wall
On South Deeside Road,
The slalom of the Dee behind us,
The sky a May Day blue.

(Beside the red phone box
In which we yelped at the Lourdes Group girls
After lights out –
Having crouched through undergrowth
In Balaclavas –
Ramming in tens,
Wrestling for the receiver...)

Aberdeen was license,
As much as five-day fluff
Could pull the wool over license-holder's eyes,
Thinking then an open-necked shirt
And gold cross & chain
Made us somehow Seventies adult.

*

One time one
Of the girls came.
We met her off the Glasgow bus:
Ties coiled in pockets,
Hair wet and scraped back
Like L.A. pimps.

The beach was warming up for the season:
A blonde head blown-dry
Atop a stripy windbreaker,
A beach-ball dam-bursting its way
To the timber groyne;

Small tankers moving all day
On the line where blue
Became a shade lighter,
Like targets no-one hit;
The black spires of three rigs
Dotted distantly.

He was winning:
Nimbler at the tomfoolery
Girls fall for, or boys fall for
Girls falling for.
His party trick
Was *making* me blush:
Hissing like a punctured bladder
Till I crimsoned,
All to Cathy's gut-cramping delight.

I hung on
(Blushing at the jibe green and hairy)
And belched the lager
Dermy so heroically had acquired.
Leaning back against the sea-wall,
He exhaled smugly
Through his nose...

At benediction,
Windswept and queasy on thurible,
(Having just about
Kept it down up

The back of the riotous bus)
Divine Praises ran on forever…

I swung the red-hot charcoal ever wider,
Gagging on incense;
Swaying bone-dry
In the stare of the cold white eye
Of the wavy-rayed golden monstrance.

IN CARMEL

'Just turned twenty-four,' I overheard,
'World at her feet...' The scent of white roses
Lingered, and, shockingly, the stubborn whiff
Of the disembodied community.

In the cobbled yard, bright with tablecloths,
The Irish chaplain, feeding cherrycake
Into his sticky mouth, canted over:
'Would you like to *see* her?'I blushed, nodding.

In the dim parlour, pale behind iron grilles,
She suffered cousins and sickly perfumes.
It felt like queuing up for confession:
The trite list; only one thing on your mind...

THE FATHER'S TALE

The way she told me as well,
Like 'I'm away to the shops'
Or 'Dad, lend us a tenner
Till the weekend' Dead simple.
Just came out with it that night,
Not long after she was home.
Cathy was back doing shifts.

For the first time in my life,
I hit her. It was just...shock.
I didn't know where to turn.
I could've coped with most things,
The usual things – a wean,
A Proddy boyfriend *(any*
Boyfriend), bad debts, drugs even,
But this...I'd never even

Thought, didn't bat an eyelid
That last break, she brought her pal,
Her flat-mate, she said. Zoe.
One of these feminist types –
Punk hair, a good bit older
Than Maggie. And her saying
They'd be fine in her old room.
Jesus! Right under my nose.

She was always that...normal,
You know? Used to come out
A lot with me and her mother,
Down the club. Few jars, a dance.
Not many lads but so what?

Just waiting till she's ready.
At least she's no slag, I thought.

She moved to London. London!
Figures. She did well for herself.
Got a wee flat, a shared thing.
Kept mentioning this Zoe.
My friend Zoe, she would say.
So whose fault is it? Eh? Mine?
Was it me somehow? I mean,
How does a lassie be*come*...

That *word*. I keep hearing it.
And all this AIDS business.
I mean, do women get it
As well? I've started watching
These programmes. There's nobody
To ask, is there? The Church? Aye,
The old Canon wouldn't miss
Me and hit the wall, would he?

Maybe it's a phase, to do
With hormones 'n that, maybe
She'll grow...God, she's twenty-two,
Twenty-three! What did she say?
Since she was eighteen? What's that,
Five years? All that time.
All that time I'd no idea.
You should have *stayed*, Maggie love.

RETREAT

Tadhg slid the *Gordons* out of his cassock,
And crystal tumblers, muffled in tissue.
What better libation for Good Friday?

Their talk, in the tingle of gin, drifted
To the intricate pleasures of the flesh,
The secrets of a dappled day in bed...

A floorboard creaked outside: scrotum-stapling.
Vigilance
                passed on down the corridor.
Liberality near wept with relief.

A lifetime to the day, on the stroke of three –
One a monsignor, the other widower –
The moment fizzed in their heads like tonic.

WHAT-IS-THE-CASE

A back seat hard on the buttocks,
The kneeler no more forgiving;
Looking up, the tabernacle's
Unforeshortened, spot-lit Emmaus.

A weak bell, shuffling to feet.
Jump-cut to the consecration
When, glasses off, the parish priest
Goes down in a snort of Latin.

The old boy fumbles with the gong
As atoms hold on to themselves.
Outside before the end, morning:
The river slate-grey, mountains black;

The noises of children playing.

AT SEA

In Oban I changed my life.
From cassocks and post-prandial strolls

To hungover kitchens
And dog's abuse from the Spanish chef;

Butter-fingered, blushing,
Bewildered by fourteen-hour days;

The butt of Lancastrian
Breakfast table one-liners.

'It'll never happen, lad.'
It had. And where could I turn?

*

The staff tireless and rampant,
I usually called it a night

And felt my way down corridors
Rolling in the heavy swell –

Shoes left out to attention,
Diplomatic bags of laundry;

A low of pleasure from somewhere
Behind wafer-thin walls –

Praying for the landfall
Of a day off, with money in my pocket.

*

In bed, stoned, I wrote home
A breezy letter – *everything's fine!* –

Turned over and was out cold,
Till a giggly thump and 'Ssssht!'

It was Rab, back from the disco,
Breathing booze into the small room:

'You awake, pal?'

A TALKING TO

'There's not much
To say,' I said,
Hating this,
'Don't you think?'

The faces
On the mantelpiece
Maintained a dis-
approving stare.

The tape stopped.
Ursula stirred
On my lap and leapt
Over to you,

Where you sat
In your black dress,
Legs crossed, shoes
Kicked off, swirling

A glass of brandy
Intently; then looked
Straight at me:
'You are so frightened

Of anything
That involves...risk!'
God, here we go.
A talking to.

Bloody talk.
Why can't we keep it

All warm and dark…
And coy?

You stood up,
Smiling, your hand out
For my glass; took it
To the sideboard.

Your shoulders
Moved in a small sigh;
Turning, drink in hand:
'You're such a *boy*.'

AT A WEDDING IN BAWTRY, 1991

Sitting up, you really flinched when I daubed
Your pitted cheek with TCP.
                                        Dispatched
To the off-license for red wine and sweets,
I clicked on the portable, for the news.

A crumpled Union Jack in breathless air;
Victorious Paras, in khaki, swarming
Over a Chieftain's glistening hard-on –
Splayed supplements on our twin room floor.

ONE LESS

All the time she talked about her mother,
Whose mission in life was to get her married
Into the right family; the latest
Was vetted for background and salary,
Which bombed me right out: Catholic student
With a one syllable Irish surname.
She talked about her father and her brothers,
Her grandmother, who listened to her,
Her friends, of course, and her friends' boyfriends;
And *her* boyfriends, which was the worst of it.
I never did get used to that, hearing
Her discuss so-and-so and look at me
As if I was to give an opinion.
That never seemed to bother her at all.
It bothered me all right. I used to think,
If she's telling me all this about them,
What do the rest of them know about me?
It was a different world. Anyway,
The whole thing lasted about three months;
And when it was pretty much all over,
I turned up at the flat for dinner
And told her, before she set the table,
That I really thought we should finish it.
She was perfect: she called me a lowlife
And wished me a slow death from stomach cancer,
Stormed about the room and slammed the door
Said I could bloody well starve then
And cried and went and stood by the window.
Five minutes later she gave me a hug
And made me promise we'd always be friends.
Sure. I left the flat and took a right towards
The routine pleasures of Dumbarton Road;

Leaving her to it, leaving her one less
To worry about, one less to worry.
Though there were, I remember, moments
When I fell for the whole scenario:
Taking a half-pissed walk in the twilight
Through Kelvingrove park, picking off leaves,
Reading aloud from our book of erotic verse;
And she would give me a sideways look and smile,
As if she knew exactly what that did to me.

MOURNER

A grey-haired,
Long-coated priest,
Draped in purple stole;
The book closed,

A slowed-down
Sign of the cross
Over the fresh grave;
Grave-diggers

Standing by
Shifting in the cold,
Stooping to breathe life
Into cupped hands;

The widow
Huddled away,
Her little dry sobs
Half comical.

The doldrums
Lifted as we filed
Into St Lawrence's Club
For refreshments:

A young lad
Balancing a tray
Of whiskies; a spread
By the Legion.

I sat down
With a sausage roll

And a wee half; turning
To the old dear

Asking my name,
I caught the widow's eye
In the wall-mirror:
Asking the same.

LAST TRAIN

First, we sorted out who I was.
'No, not the skip-hire Friels.'
The driver knew my grandfather, then.
'We used to call him the Kaiser,'
He said, staring straight ahead
Into the rapidly-approaching night.
'That's going back a bit, mind you.
Way back.' For maybe a minute
No one spoke. The driver's substantial
Bulk on the flip-down seat
Rocked gently to the train's rhythm,
His grip loose on the dead man's handle.
A half-smile appeared on his face
But still no one said anything.
The guard whistled idly through the paper.
Outside the shapes of pine trees
Accelerated and slowed behind us.
The lights of a cluster of houses
Came and went in the blinking
Of an eye. We hurtled through
A closed station, a porter
With his back to us raising a hand
As he locked up for the night.
I'd woken up at the end of the line,
Half cut, totally bewildered.
They were going back to Paisley
To park the train. They'd give me a lift.
'So why the Kaiser?' I said finally.
He laughed through his nose
And re-settled on the seat. 'Because
He ran that depot like a tyrant,
That's why,' he said, half turning.

'One time I showed up late for back shift.
I had a wee drink in me, like.'
The guard tutted: 'Bad news man.'
'He nearly bloody throttled me.
Literally. They had to drag him off.
He was like that. Too wound up.
You never saw him down the club.
It was just work and then home.
By the book. That was Frankie.
He was a good union man though.
Apparently the management hated
Having to deal with him. He was a mule
Round that negotiating table.
He wouldn't budge. Would not retire
Neither. It took about four
Gold watches to get rid of him.
My cousin, Tam, got him a wee number
In the yards' 'The *yards?*''Aye,
Just odd jobs, sorta style.
I mean he was nearly seventy.
He made the men their tea,
Made sure there was clean towels,
Went for the papers an' that.
They give him a coupla quid.
Buckshee. He was quite happy.'
There was silence for five beats.

'Did you not know that?' said the driver.
'I knew about the watches,' I said.

THE DOLPHINS AT CULLEN

We bought Diet Cokes and sat in the car,
Listening to the forecast. It was bleak.

On the blunt headland to our right,
The prison cell where John MacLean

Held out in the heyday of Red Clydeside,
Force fed to stave off martyrdom.

On through drizzly wee towns
You wonder could you live in ever again,

Down Pennan's slippery slope
To the phone box where a yuppie

Sang the praises of Scottish air
To Burt Lancaster in his penthouse office.

Lungs tingling, shaded eyes
Escorted a cargo ship heading east;

Then Cullen. We'd come for the dolphins
And sat on different peaks,

Waiting. A cormorant joined in.
Dark clouds piled high over the Moray Firth.

But there was no sign; no harbinger
High-tailing it over the waves.

VISITING HOUR

The gearbox brayed
On the brow of the hill.
Tipped ash swirled around me
As the doors hissed open.

Inhaling pure relief,
I dawdled on the drive,
Stretching in the play
Of boneless fingers of light.

In the hall a hotplate
Glided past, unloaded;
Tribes of spray on the move
Under a neon sky.

At her stagnant bedside,
I pulled a chair right in:
Her swollen left hand un-
clutched and limp by her side;

My smiling photograph
In its black oval frame
(Holding the red degree
Like I'm playing rounders);

The intestinal pile
Of her rosary beads;
The vase that 'looked better';
The tulips' *Consumatum Est.*

HOGMANAY

At the bells
We stood up stiffly
And tinged the cut crystal
To the new year.

Dad slipped off
To sprinkle the rooms
(And anyone in them)
With holy water.

Left in peace,
I breathed in
At the open window
Where the night used to be so full

Of ships' horns
Blasting the sky
With gargantuan flatulence;
Blurred close encounters.

Tonight, though,
Merely a sad pamp
Lingers a moment
Over the town.

Lights go out;
Somewhere the river
Wrinkles in the dark,
Prowling west.

The dead shift
Under its cold pelt,

Dulse-entangled.
They will not come back

Transfigured
In half-lit, creepy tales.
We don't go in
So much for myths,

Believing more
Often than not,
That life's exactly
What it looks like.

DAVYDEEP
(Being an alphabetical list, or litany, of Clyde shipwrecks
from 1770 to the present day)

Aber
Acorn
Admiral
Aimwell
Albion

Argyll
Atalanta
Auchmountain
Aura
Aurora

Baltic
Belle Adventure
Beta
Briton
Bruce

Caitloch
Caros
Caroline
Carrick
Castle Hill

City of Madras
Clan Campbell
Clio
Clyde
Comet II

Mother of Christ, star of the sea,
Pray for the wand'rer, pray for me

Daisy
Daisy
Dart
Dolphin
Dreamland

Eliza
Ellen Ann
Emily
Eugine
Europa

Firth of Cromarty
Flying Scud
Gleaner
Gloriana
Golden Effort

Harriet Julia
Harmony
Hope
Ianthe
Iona

Mother of Christ, star of the sea,
Pray for the wand'rer, pray for me

Ithuriel
Jane
Janet
Jeannie Blair
Jubilee

Lady Mary
Lairdselm
Lairdsmoor

Lakemoor
Laurel

Liverpool
Lizzie Gardner
Loch Etive
Longway
Louise

Maid of Orleans
Marjorie Seed
Matchless
Mocking Bird
Mona

Nith
Otter
Pearl
Pliedes
Portland

Mother of Christ, star of the sea,
Pray for the wand'rer, pray for me

Queen of May
Rambler
Reaper
Rowan
Sea Bird

Socrates
Solway Queen
Splendid
Springbok
Sprite

Storm Lights
Strathdee
Strathgarry
Strathspey
Sutherland

U-33
Ulysses
Urd
Valkyrie
Vandal

Vestal
Victoire
Vivo
Wild Duck
Winsome

Mother of Christ, star of the sea,
Pray for the wand'rer, pray for me

MOVING

Our sum of worldly goods packed
In the rented van, the farewell scene
Was fumbling, mute. You turned the key:

Wipers waved. The rubber plant,
At least, made you smile: big-eared,
Upright in clutter, clowning around

As we swung on to the main road,
Untensing in our high-up seats,
Windows down, lighting cigarettes.

A snake of slow lights
Wound round the pine-silhouetted hill.
The sky was cut with molten red.

We'd no tapes, no radio.
'Why don't you *sing* to me,' you said,
Turning quickly, eyes delighted

With the novelty. I mulled,
Then tried a few, self-consciously,
Faltering after the first lines.

'I've always meant to learn those songs...'
And you: 'I guess there's no demand
For that kind of stuff.' So we sat –

Gusts of wind tugging our hair,
The dark shapes of the countryside
Slipping past at various speeds –

With no singing, or talking.

CONTENT

A Volvo sluicing puddles into light
(Like wings) in a lush Highland valley;

A bronzed family trotting from the surf,
Their broad smiles chalky as white cliffs;

A playschool bungalow and spiky sun,
Levitating scarecrow-girl out front:

The silver blur of a train obliter-
ated them, in a panning shot towards

What I'd hoped, until I saw my grey-haired
Lugubrious mien in the window

Stopping slowly like a wheel of fortune
Past the glittering prize, would be content.

NORTH KENSINGTON

A helicopter, small as a hawk,
Tracks its scuttling prey on film.
Wildflowers bend in the traffic's breeze
On banks of stagnant Astroturf.
A bearded glare points from a poster:
THE LORD WANTS YOU...*To skin up man,*
Added in aerosol. Ragga throbs
From a cabriolet, the driver noosed
With gold, alien in ray-bans.
Noise pursues him down the street.
The lights change anyway.
A highflat's tinfoil side is sunset,
A brownstone is the horizon.
An old dear with stripy shopping
Frowns at a thought she nearly had.
To be is not to be perceived...

My dinner boiling in the bag,
I work away my tie, tear up
The plastic window CONGRATULATIONS,
Uncork the flavour of the month
And slump into my sofa-bed view
Of motorways on top of motorways...
The vertical a highflat spiky
With satellite dishes, stamen erect.
Someone drifts to a sink;
Another cleans a window
With slow repeated waves
That go unanswered.

PLAYING TENNIS IN THE SHADOW OF MOUNT CARMEL

With such a canopy of blue sky
And cries of 'pasa!' from the football game
Swarming around the base of the flats,
A *Real* strip flapping on a balcony,
It could've been a poor neighbourhood in Madrid
In the dead centre of summer,
Not Little Vatican, London,
In the End Days that proved the cranks correct,
With the atmosphere soon to be panic-seized,
Then waterlogged with remorse.

You just wouldn't have known to look at the sky,
Or the warm tarmac with its pentacle
Of vivid bylines, the holed compound fence,
Seats left out by the staff at lunchtime,
Or the torpid state of my attention
As I umpired slumped in a bucket chair
While Nick and Peter staggered from deuce
To advantage, and so on interminably;
Behind us, the medieval walls
Of Carmel, which also would sunder
And the brides of Christ come into the daylight,
Asking in the first place: 'Who won?'

FOOD OF LOVE

Two stops from work, we ordered 'just the one'
Snug by the real fire in pre-rush hour
El Metro – outnumbered by spruce waiters
Flapping dish towels at each other's groins.
Trains spilled bad-tempered souls; the bar filled up.
Six later, the *Sevillanas* thundered
On the toughened dais, and we were red
With horny fantasies drink had let slip.

At the Christmas 'do', our first grown-up date,
I turned sour at the gladsome jigs and reels,
And Veronica Ball, who'd been to Skye
And valued 'the music of the people'.
The cab driver slid the partition shut
On the foul-mouthed cadences of our row.

WORK

A proselyte, or headcase, or loser
Shoulders a life-size cross up Ladbroke Grove.
He's routine as tantrums and trafficking.

Schoolchildren, high on freedom, wrestle
Each other to the ground – resilient, light
On their feet, as yet unencumbered

By the shape of a life, more like work than love,
You one day realise you're carrying...
When the surge of a red bus over

The brow of the hill is sweetness in your veins;
And the whack of a branch on the top deck
Is the soul, mortally tired, crying *No*.

SEEING THE RIVER

A rumbling, then a real wind, preceded
The rupture and peopled strobe of the Tube...

Doors butted shut. There were seats to spare
That mid-afternoon in late September;

A few old folk heading home from lunch clubs,
Girny toddlers, mothers lost in magazines.

My briefcase at heel, we clattered gently
Into a smeared, sudden daylight of rooftops

And squint aerials; crossed Putney Bridge
At a cautionary ten miles per hour,

The power cutting, revving, then cutting.
I cramped with regret, seeing the river

At low tide through the iron lattice-work...
For a time after Finals when I walked

Miles, muttering quotes, and ended up
On the dulse-clotted beach at Cardwell Bay,

Chucking skimmers onto the placid Clyde:
Armed, adroit, absorbed, unaccountable.

IN TURKEY

The corrugated shack
By the side of the road
Was, explained the barman
Over yet more raki,
Having dealt with Islam
And National Service,
A barber's. His cousin

Came up from the city
For the tourist season.
He worked and slept there,
Tried to save a little...
'We will go tomorrow, '
We said, like royalty
Bestowing patronage.

Fragile, we breakfasted
Lightly in the shade.
The barman, serving tea,
Gently reminded us.
'All *right*.' We trudged along
For a shave. In the dust
Two boys chased a football.

We went inside, waited.
An unmade bed, posters
Of English football teams.
He came to the doorway:
Out of breath, uncertain,
His body close to us;
His hand at last: '*please, sir*.'

FATHER AND SON

Unbearably buoyant the night before
My return to Blairs, I'd be brought back down
To earth by Dad's Polonius routine.
He'd been there in the black-and-white Forties,
And had to leave, he said, only because...

Now, in the grey-skied secular Nineties,
Home with a girlfriend who's not a Catholic,
I psych myself for one of our wee talks.
A curt 'she's lovely,' though, is not the fierce
Sectarian wrangle I'd predicted.

Thin-armed in his vest, fishing a tea-bag
Out of a garish SCOTTISH POWER mug,
He turns to theology... the garden
He's pottered in since the leaden handshake.
'It's the only chance I get,' he mock pleads.

I'm beat but listen, behind the big sighs
I always did; deep down, like him,
A believer in the examined life; and God knows
He's put the hours in: steeling himself
For the strange revelations of the king.

KITCHEN

High on a votive shelf,
Mary of Medjugorje:

PRAY FOR US SINNERS
Scratched on the pedestal;

For nine days bottom-lit
By a jittery fat red candle.

On the battered portable,
In drained colour, the news:

Lorries in convoy ghosting
Through wooded hills.

Sightings in the village.

BIG FOUR O

Lodged
In the corner,
I scanned the untouched savouries,
Gulping Beaujolais.

Children,
Briefly radiant at the door,
Drove a hard bargain
For being good...

They looked well:
This loosened-up generation,
Far travelled in the land
Of Zappa.

Now in V-necks
And lace blouses, warm with wine,
The knots unravelled
To hear tell

Of weans puking
In cars, dormers
And paid help; t'ai chi at the Poly,
Who's cheating who;

The dream,
Tonight so palpable,
Of just selling up and hitching
To Skye, say, or Lewis...

The risk
Of holding on to hips

As the house juddered underfoot:
I LOVE YOU BAY-BEE!

Our coats found,
We ventured into the swaying night;
Gifts of moist cake
In our hands.

DOLE TOWN

Car parks gleaming in sunshine
Where miles of shipyards were.
A whole way of life, as it's now called,
Closed with no comment;

A cheque, just, cashed on a party
To end all parties, world cruise
And real stone fire surround (no shares
Portfolio will keep you warm).

The walking heart attacks,
Whose speeches brought them out in droves,
Are down the dole asking lassies
Their daughter's age to translate this;

Giro day and labourers loiter
In the Well Park with carry-outs;
Loud, obstreperous in the cold,
Trailing home steamin' the back a five.

In schemes shouts like gunshots carry
Through the damp crepuscular air;
Kids on the big-puddled wasteground
Experiment with Swiss army knives.

At night time a silence the town
Has never known; distant squad cars'
Whooping American sirens;
A drunk cursing the state he's in.

WELDER

A welder in his forties, from the Port,
Leans, bored, on a supermarket trolley.
He can see the future: VOID IN PROGRESS.

The Queen will visit Greenock tomorrow
To re-open the Custom House; the cost
Of landscaping the route is undisclosed.

The former welder, going on fifty,
Pulls the blinds shut on a blare of sunlight,
Blips the tele on and unzips his stash.

ENTERPRISE ZONE

Demolition is booming.
A FRIEL's skip stands alone

In acres of rubble,
Like a fortified pub.

Seagulls waddle, and stare...
Waiting for opening time.

*

The shell of the rope factory
Is a Cretan amphitheatre.

A wildflower belts it out
For the adoring grass.

*

The Custom House is back
From holiday, fit and tanned;

Doric columns
Pleased with their hairdo.

A hunchback in his gaberdine
Peering into the river

Could be John Galt,
His heart in the Mediterranean.

*

Saplings stand around
The landscaped site

Like shivering souls
Bare to the Westerly;

Benches with wee plaques
Gleaming like monocles.

Rigged up on stilts
An artist's impression

Of the waterfront
Come the millennium:

Sepia-toned, botanical,
Vaulted in plate glass.

*

The stadium lights,
Like packets of Aspirin,

Illuminate the scratches of rain,
Whorled by wind.

The rainwater evacuates,
Head first down the nearest drain;

The new insurance building
Berths at quayside.

KEIR HARDIE STREET

I was lifted up
To see my grandfather return

From Cappielow:
Cloth-capped, canny,

Whistling a jig
Through the fine rain.

He flourished boiled sweets
From behind my ears,

Over and over,
As he did to Mum, home

From the 'dark years'
In America;

My grandmother at his back:
Dry-eyed; waiting.

*

Devils raved
Behind the translucent skin

Of the *Sunday Post*
Sucked on to the mouth of the grate.

Arthur Montford
Flickered in the corner:

A droning post-mortem
On the game.

For my sins
I was wedged

Between parents,
Holding my tongue.

*

After tea I waded
Into the long grass out the back,

'Don't go far!'
Ringing in my ears.

I took the plunge
And kicked out for the bottom

Through glancing
Vocative shoals,

Dialects of sea-horse
And mussel,

To find John Dory,
Whose home

Is the long-haired hulls,
The dream-boats of the deep;

Only to falter
At the first sound from above –

My mother's sharp cry
Calling me in.

WORKING-CLASS POET

Someone else had set the thing up.
She never had the time these days.
All the features editor told her
Was the Holiday Inn at 12
To meet some poet. The next big thing,
Apparently. Whitbread. Television.
Set text. She'd never liked poetry...

Afternoons drowsing over Wordsworth, Keats.
Something about pathetic fallacy.
(Funny how some phrases stick.)
She'd read nothing by what's-his-name.
Sod it. She'd have enough in no time:
Difficult background; the drinking;
Wild eyes. No problem.

She sat in the piano music
Of the lobby; a large gin, dead,
On the low table by her knee.
'Same again?' She smiled weakly back
At the porter and leant forward
To fold her cigarette into
Extinction. 12:47.

NEW YEAR'S DAY
(for Richard Price)

Peering into the morgue white of the fridge
At liver pâté moulding on a plate,
The best my brain could muster was a drive...
The hills, as we manoeuvred round pot-holes
At a ridiculous ten miles per hour,
Mourned it seemed in drifting skeins of black rain;
Occasional trees were etched like martyrs
On grey sky; the river boiled with vengeance.
Slumped in the front seat sucking Evian,
I pointed feebly at this or that thing.
Fresh, proprietorial in a cramped
Row in the back, Liu yelped with delight
When maybe-a-fox streaked across the road.
Largs was post-Apocalyptic (it had
A quiet one); Nardini's was open,
Luminous against the moors like a liner
Steaming west in mossgreen Atlantic swell.
A few in steerage scowled from their card games
As we trooped to the far corner, my guests
Nodding at the somnolent string quartet,
The Thirties decor. We formed a circle
Round the glass-topped, too-small wicker table.
I looked through the padded menu, ordered
Sorbets and, with a tremor, Russian tea;
My coat still on, a bloodless hand clamped
On the table, squinting through the chatter
To the Gents; the room heaving heavenwards
As Charlie's violin scraped into
Abide With Me, 'for the dear departed...'

ALMA MATER

Collared with scarves, we rooted privately
In the unkempt formal garden,
Where, in fourth year, I'd flounced on the lawn
In lurid make-up and apron
For the dress rehearsal photo-session,
Flirting like a real Highland queen.

On the Green stairs, the doleful Madonna
And her plump, precocious Christ
Were still framed in flaking gilt baroque:
A timeless ennui above
The morning stampede of dishevelled boys,
Wee Ben hounding the stragglers.

At my old room, I knocked for some reason…
Glare of mustardseed and blue sky,
Then a fusty glory-hole of bedsteads,
A mattress shot in the stomach;
The speckled formica table, dust-dimmed,
Where I poured out my bleeding heart.

Janet teased the mood, kept the chill off…
But floors creaked with midnight sortees,
Tunnel corridors had ghosts of late boys;
And the bare-shelved Lady altar
Where I muttered decade after decade
In a dream-haze of piety

Moved me, and set a distance between us
As I sunk into nostalgia.
There was silence in the car as we turned
Onto a wet South Deeside Road.

Ahead of us a dour night on the town,
Nursing pints in the Vale of Tears.

REAL WORLD
(i.m. D.C.M., 1962-1984)

In the stepped rows of razor partings –
A backdrop of tufty grass and blue sky –
I quickly find your just-up hairdo,
The clot of sellotape at the hinge
Of National Health beatnik spectacles...

Easy with languages, you teased
My ham-fisted Latin with a gravitas
I bristled at, and wouldn't elucidate
The risky-looking motto gouged in your desk –
Nolite te bastardes carborundorum.

Your volte-face, the day you went to Perth
To win the Schools' Maths Prize and got back late,
Matured by six pints and Leith Girls High.
Lighting your second smoke
In the crumbling cottage, until then
Our unviolated noust, our boys' den,
You said that you had heard the language
Of the 'real world' beyond our seminary walls...

Years later, I found you in the Union bar,
Constructing spliffs on *Criminal Law Vol I,*
A gulped-at pint of Guinness in front of you.
I'd slept in till midday. 'You're learning, Freddy,'
You ribbed, eyes blazing with cheap lenses,
Tweaking the end to a pedantic point.

What you learn now, dear shade, is untranslatable.

BALMEDIE BEACH

The four of us, leaden-calved, hands at throats,
Headed for the pill-box, half uprooted
Out of the sand, its concrete legs showing,
Tilted back like a crash-landed capsule.

Dozens of footprints scurried from the door;
A pile of syringes an offering,
No doubt, to whatever god they worshipped,
Since ritual follows revelation.

We boarded the dim claustrophobic bridge:
Like ducking into a helicopter.
The windows framed angled, sliding seascapes;
Nausea gripped us by the jugular.

ABROAD
(for Martin and Maggie)

Guzzling Caesars
In the hissing swelter of the gas fire,
We dutifully sat
Through the albums of Canada,
The black stray *Lucky*
Coiled on the cushion between us.
Unimpressive unlinked
To memory, the thrill or gag
Of seeing *me*... a white-legged blur
Woodenly offered a hillside packed with trees;
A maybe-a-smudge a mile to port,
The showering lash of a humpback's tail!
A mofette of whale breath
A running jump away, pure evil...

*

The lasagne browned
And the Valpolicella breathed
At an unpeopled table
As mein host, my oldest friend,
Thumped around and slammed back
In with *Nagano 1990*...
On the brink in the karaoke bar,
The foamhead microphone limp by his side,
Bared greasy teeth,
Eyes of a gorged Vlad the Impaler.
'Moments before I crashed into the P.A...'
And perhaps the morning after,
A snow-capped Hokusai,
The sky a Marian blue.

*

Jabbering abroad,
I tore open the garlic bread –
A genie puffing
From the ruptured foil,
Your eyebrow raised
To guillotine my reckless plans –
While after the fruit bowl, the Blue Label
And three hours sleep,
At the end of our long and verdant slide home,
(If home is where the rent is,
                where the job is,
                where the gyp is)
London jammed in a mucilage of lights,
Dimming towards the millennium.

The flap of the letterbox rose and fell sluggishly, once, to announce the arrival of Billy just after eight. He stood in the porchlight, suntanned and smiling in a crumpled linen suit. HELL-O! I went to shake his hand but remembered the last few times we'd met, we'd taken to hugging each other heartily like long-lost comrades (for Scots, particularly, this sort of effusiveness takes time and distance).

'Come on in! How're you doin'? '

'Fine, fine. How are you?'

He bundled in with a rucksack, a holdall bulging with bottles of wine wrapped in *La Republica,* and, for some reason, a pound of fresh garlic, which provided an occasional and surreal talking point until he left.

It was mild enough to sit out on the patio, laid earlier in the summer by our jack-of-all-trades neighbour, Mark. It was small, the borders unkempt: a concrete poem to our lack of interest or knowledge in the natural processes of the garden. Not that much would've grown. The soil was little more than clotted mud and behind us was the railway. The grime generated by the trains settled on everything with alarming speed and density, like invisible black rain.

I brought out a bottle of chilled wine and two glasses. With a twinge of guilt, and a new sensation of atavistic content, I drank the wine down in gulps as we blethered in the Southfields twilight. Every so often a Tube train thundered past in a blur of grey metal and milky light, muting the volume of our conversation. An ironically twee 'Sweet-heart!' summoned me to the kitchen. I set the table with paper napkins and cutlery, and opened one of the newly-arrived bottles. Three steaming platefuls under our noses, the evening got under way with small moans of appreciation and the passing round and breaking of fresh bread.

Plonked in the centre of the shoogly plastic table was a miniature Doric column topped with a stout red candle. In the light of the single flame, at chin height, we looked like Hammer Horror conspirators, belying the levity of our conversation. Billy's enthusiasm for Rome seemed to have wilted little in the daily 100 degree heat and the soaked and sleepless nights. There was a fresh round of predictably outrageous drinking stories involving Neapolitan firewater, a group of Irish pilgrims, and a gruesome vignette from an underfunded Italian Health Service. His repartee was as vivid and infectious as ever, a cigarette constantly in one hand as he chopped and swotted the air in the heat of narrative. I envied his stage presence and unflagging stamina for sociability.

We met at University as post-graduate students. He had come down from Glasgow, where we had the same tutor, the year before. I was making tea in the communal kitchen of Exeter House – the rabbit warren which was home for the two years of my last fling in academia – when he walked straight in and asked: Are you Raymond Friel? I felt that a *yes* might elicit a handgun from his brown, scuffed leather jacket and a bullet or two into the cranium. He didn't seem well disposed to the idea of meeting me. I had a bottle of gin in my room from which I'd been tippling since my arrival to stave off the effects of loneliness. I asked if he wanted a drink. An hour later, with the gin finished and the room dense with cigarette smoke, we had hit it off, discovering a mutual interest in decadence, poetry and being Scottish; that we were from either side of the Great Sectarian Divide lent a keener anthropological and spiritual edge to our budding friendship: we had much to learn from each other. The session continued in *The Magdalen Arms*.

Seven years after that memorable night of first acquaintance, dinner having been consumed to exuberant praise, all three of us well on the road to oblivion, it was time, I thought, with the vigorous and unanswerable inspiration of too much drink, for the wedding video. I ignored Billy's pleading sideways look. I hadn't properly forgiven him for missing our big day. He'd been up to no good in the north of Italy with a party of rich American students. This was revenge of a kind. The video itself was an amateur affair shot by an in-law, who'd only bought the camera the week before and was vague on the finer points of film-making.

Settled into the darkness, we watched as blizzard gave way abruptly to moving pictures of ourselves. The camera bobbed its way through the mêlée of guests in the hotel lobby; lingered inexplicably on the ersatz oval of cherubs and clouds on the ceiling; panned along the top table oblivious of the blurred heads and hats in the foreground; and, at one point, swept towards the carpet as if the centre of consciousness in that quirky but memorable narrative had given up the ghost and keeled over. There were, however, successful moments, including a steady pan of our progress through the whoops of delight to the place of honour; a close up of myself and Janet deep in conversation over coffee. No doubt I was moaning at the prospect of the bridal waltz, which we'd rehearsed at home to no avail. It was the one thing which had bugged me all day, like grit in my shoe. In the event, Janet steered my left feet round the polished dance floor through 360 degrees of exploding flash bulbs and the ebb and flow of warm applause.

'To la dolce vita!' said Billy, suddenly, from the other side of the room, and raised a tumbler half-full of Glenmorangie; he put it to his lips, and drank it down until it was finished.

HUSBAND

Three days married, I held on to you
As you succumbed to the bone-tiredness
We both felt, the whole city felt.

The Ca d'oro was under wraps,
Like a fiend being ushered into court;
Flashes glancing off the tarpaulin.

Past the Guggenheim, the tumid Angel
On horseback on the patio, arms open wide
As if in ecstasy, or shot in the back.

You blinked awake, from dreams or discomfort,
And for a split-second looked with fright,
As if you'd never in your life laid eyes on me.

THE RIGHT NOTE

In the Jesuit church a tinny voice
Hammered through high mass,
Undeterred by ripples of response.

Querulous gulls circled high overhead.
Fettered gondolas slapped at the water,
Their silver snouts reaching up for titbits.

Composed between creaky mooring posts,
A muffled stranger focusing our smiles
Into the past (but not your right thumb hooked

In my back pocket), I could've just sung,
Or *said* something; and nearly did, but for the fear
Of just missing the right note.

DAKIN WARD

Stoned women
Haunt the corridors,
Gowns half-open
In siesta heat.

In the late afternoon,
Men come gauchely
With armfuls of praise
And fruit no one wants.

SPRING

Tiny in the basin of blue, a plane
Dreams of America, leaving no trail.

Flocculent clouds snag on the gold-nippled,
Green copper dome of the London mosque.

The imam's hermenuetics is tannoyed
To the faithful, cross-legged in the car park.

White as blossom, the blank page incites me –
But I have no nascent universal song,

Merely a fondness for particulars,
And a certain way with necessity.

Downstairs, pale as a Botticelli,
You dab at a still life of apples and pears.

THE BOAT HOUSE AT LAUGHARNE

A plummy Charles Laughton voice
(A late recording)

Inhabits the low-beamed
Cabin of a front room.

A Fern Hill tea-towel wrinkles
Over the hearth.

'He was a right bastard to his wife,'
You said, and left.

Outside, I peered into the writing shed:
Cut off, cosy;

From the rickety desk, a dazzling view
Of Towy estuary;

Postcards of poets on the lintel,
A Van Gogh chair;

Scrunched up papers by the stove
For the credulous,

As if he'd chucked it and headed off
For a swift one...

Below, you picked your way
Carefully over the rocks.

EASTER SUNDAY

A mile out of Laugharne our hired Fiesta
Shuddered in perfunctory death-rattle,
Slid backwards into the lay-by, and died
With its bonnet jutting east at rainclouds.

Ratty after a few pints and no lunch,
We traipsed in single file back into town
Clutching plastic bags of remaindered
Biographies and souvenir thimbles...

Past the low-slung sitting rooms of King Street –
TVs flickering behind lace curtains;
A police car parked outside Brown's Hotel,
Bleary drinkers blinking into daylight.

In the phone box, static cracked between us.
With the chirp of each unanswered spondee,
I wished us back to a dappled morning
When, in bed, we'd compromised about church,

Saved on the car hire and thumbed a lift,
Wandered over a muddy Sir John's Hill
With the estuary spread out below us;
And a glimpse of the town's little graveyard

Had brought to mind Stanley Spencer's
The Resurrection: Port Glasgow, in which
The dead clamber out of the cold ground
To embrace their loved ones, and give praise.